MARIANNE
FAITHFULL

WITH DAVID DALTON

YEAR ONE

PENGUIN BOOKS

PENGUIN BOOKS

Published by the Penguin Group. Penguin Books Ltd, 27 Wrights Lane, London w8 5TZ, England. Penguin Books USA Inc., 375 Hudson Street, New York, New York 10014, USA. Penguin Books Australia Ltd, Ringwood, Victoria, Australia. Penguin Books Canada Ltd, 10 Alcorn Avenue, Toronto, Ontario, Canada M4V 3B2. Penguin Books (NZ) Ltd, 182–190 Wairau Road, Auckland 10, New Zealand · Penguin Books Ltd, Registered Offices: Harmondsworth, Middlesex, England · This extract is from *Faithfull* first published in Great Britain by Michael Joseph 1994. This edition published 1996. Copyright © Marianne Faithfull 1994. All rights reserved · The moral right of the author has been asserted · Typeset by Rowland Phototypesetting Ltd, Bury St Edmunds, Suffolk. Printed in England by Clays Ltd, St Ives plc · Except in the United States of America, this book is sold subject to the condition that it shall not, by way of trade or otherwise, be lent, re-sold, hired out, or otherwise circulated without the publisher's prior consent in any form of binding or cover other than that in which it is published and without a similar condition including this condition being imposed on the subsequent purchaser · 10 9 8 7 6 5 4 3 2 1

CONTENTS

Courtfield Road

It's the summer of 1966, but for me it is Year One. I've been adopted by Brian and Anita, and their flat in Courtfield Road has become my second home. I'm trying to make a beeline there, but everywhere I look there's some insane distraction; Bengalis selling scarves with magic signs on them, two buskers in Elizabethan rags playing hurdy-gurdies and tiny drums, a couple of hustlers selling knock-offs of those big plastic Biba bracelets. God, will you look at David Bailey with that little tart on his arm! Harrods looming up like a great liner, and a little further on, Walton Street with dozens of seductive boutiques. Shop windows filled with bright Smartie colours. Miniskirts, sequinned gowns, slinky thigh-high boots, brass earrings, boas. Everything sparkling, modern, dazzling.

I am trying to suppress my natural urge to enter each and every one of these shops. Of course it's my talent for dropping several thousand pounds in forty-five minutes that chills John to the depths of his being. He never has been able to grasp the beauty of wretched excess, the poor darling. It should be obvious enough by now, even to me, that the more appalling the tour, the more ghastly the people involved, the easier it becomes to blow every shilling I made doing the damn thing.

Hmm . . . bells ringing somewhere. Probably in my head. God, what time is it? Half past five already? No, no, it can't be. Missed Deborah at El Cubano. Jesus, I've really done it this time. Must be those two dopey interviews this morning. God, did I really tell the BBC that Tom Jones was a werewolf from Aberystwyth? Why don't I think before I blurt these things out? They're going to think I'm crackers. Oh, who gives a flying fuck?

Who's that waving from across the street? Tony. My manager, Gerry Bron. 'What, darling? I can't hear you.' Christ, better just duck in here and try on that velvet-and-pearl outfit. *Ready, Steady, Go!* tomorrow. Can't exactly be seen in this frumpy thing. I'm already late, I tell myself, so what the hell . . .

Courtfield Road, Brian Jones and Anita Pallenberg's flat off Gloucester Road during the heady Paint-It-

Black summer of 1966. It's almost thirty years since I last set foot in the place. A veritable witches' coven of decadent illuminati, rock princelings and hip aristos. In my mind's eye I open the door. Peeling paint, clothes, newspapers and magazines strewn everywhere. A grotesque little stuffed goat standing on an amp, two huge tulle sunflowers, a Moroccan tambourine, lamps draped with scarves, a pictographic painting of demons (Brian's?) and decorously draped over a tatty armchair, a legendary leg – Robert Fraser's, I should guess. There's Brian in his finest Plantagenet satins, fixing us with vacant, fishy eyes. On the battered couch, an artfully reclining Keith is perfecting his gorgeous slouch. The hand gesturing in the manner of Veronese could only belong to the exquisite Christopher Gibbs, and hovering over the entire scene with single-lens-reflex-eye the invisibly ever-present photographer, Michael Cooper. At the centre, like a phoenix on her nest of flames . . . the wicked Anita. I'm here somewhere, too, looking up with hashish-glazed eyes from the Moroccan rug.

A dissolute 'Night Watch' of mid-sixties swinging London. Hipness, decadence and exquisite tailoring such as England had not seen since the 3

Restoration of Charles II. We were young, rich and beautiful, and the tide was turning in our favour. We were going to change everything, of course, but mostly we were going to change the rules. Unlike our parents, we would never have to renounce our youthful hedonism in favour of the insane world of adulthood.

Now here was a climate to which I was ideally suited. I'd always had a hard time with adults. What exactly were they? Early on I made a study of them, mistakenly assuming I would someday be one. From what I could observe of my mother, the most salient features of adulthood were smoking and drinking, and I knew I could manage those with no trouble at all (I'd always been a quick learner). It was the more arcane aspects of adulthood that eluded me: sex, money, social life, parenthood.

Consequently, at a time when my life as a grown-up should have begun, I was still very much a child. And everything that has happened to me, it's as if it happened to a child. All my attempts at growing up were really no more than a child playing make-believe. Convent girl reading forbidden books, budding bohemian, pop star, wife, mother.

Between the ages of seventeen and nineteen I shed

any number of old lives and grew new ones over-
night without any of them seeming quite real to me;
I discarded them as cavalierly as a child who moves
from one game to another. Pursued in earnest, any
one of these might have led to a reasonably happy
life. But then again, I wasn't interested in happiness,
I was looking for the Holy Grail.

And so it was that in the summer of 1966 I set
out in search of my next incarnation. I was alert
for any sign, anything that remotely resembled my
ongoing fantasy life would qualify, and Courtfield
Road was certainly that. Ever since my days at the
convent my secret heroes had been decadents,
aesthetes, doomed Romantics, mad bohemians and
opium-eaters. I devoured books by De Quincey,
Swinburne and Wilde. I cursed myself that I had
been born too late while secretly believing one never
is. I knew that out there somewhere (Chelsea was
the most likely spot), there was a cabal of like-
minded souls. And here, in the circle around Brian,
I'd found the very thing.

Desultory intellectual chitchat, drugs, hip aristocrats, languid dilettantes and high naughtiness. I
knew I was on my path! The antique dealer Christopher Gibbs was a Wildean aesthete come to life, 5

plucked straight from the opening lines of *The Picture of Dorian Grey*: 'From the corner of the divan of Persian saddle-bags on which he was lying, Lord Henry elevated his eyebrows, and looked at him in amazement through the thin blue wreaths of smoke that curled up in such fanciful whorls from his heavy opium-tainted cigarette.' That was Christopher exactly. I guess they were all a bit like that: gallery owner Robert Fraser, young Sir Mark Palmer and Tara Browne, the Guinness heir who 'blew his mind out in a car'. *Fin de siècle* King's Road dandies with Smokey Robinson on the turntable. Christopher and Robert, being gay, were even more extravagant.

It was at Courtfield Road that I got to know Anita Pallenberg. You can't begin to imagine what she was like in those days! She is the most incredible woman I've met in my life. Dazzling, beautiful, hypnotic and unsettling. Her smile – those carnivorous teeth! – obliterated everything. Other women evaporated next to her. She spoke in a baffling dada hipsterese. An outlandish Italo-Germanic-Cockney slang that mangled her syntax into surreal fragments. After a couple of sentences you became hopelessly lost. God, did she just say that? She was either putting you on or this was the Delphic oracle. You were on your own, it was all part of her sinister appeal.

I was utterly in her thrall and would have done anything for her. When I told her some years ago how in love with her I was at the time, Anita nodded like some great old Cheshire cat being brought her tribute. Another rat's tail to nail up on the barn door.

How Anita came to be with Brian is really the story of how the Stones became the Stones. She almost single-handedly engineered a cultural revolution in London by bringing together the Stones and the *jeunesse dorée*. Like many things in that era it all began with a party. Through her boyfriend, the painter Mario Schifano, Anita had become friendly with Lord Harlech's children, Jane, Julian and Victoria Ormsby-Gore, and through them she had got to know a group of young aristocrats and wealthy dilettantes. In this circle were Robert Fraser, Sir Mark Palmer, Christopher Gibbs and Tara Browne. They were all infatuated with pop stars.

The *jeunesse dorée* were in awe of this pop kingdom where young girls threw themselves at the feet 7 of yobbish dandies with guitars. Rock stars who were already parodying the decadent nobility of the past in their foppish clothing and manners were equally impressed by these young hip aristos. A union of the two later seemed inevitable, but no one had the foggiest idea how to go about it. Except for our Anita.

Anita happened to be in Germany working as a model when the Stones toured there in autumn 1965. She got backstage without much trouble and in no time at all had the whole group salivating over her. She immediately attached herself to Brian Jones. This was either love (it was), or a momentary lapse in Anita's otherwise impeccable social instincts, but it's not hard to see how this happened. Brian was in the habit of telling people, far beyond the point when anyone who knew better would believe it, that he was the 'leader of the group'. Anita, being a foreigner and an outsider, took him at his word. She returned in triumph to London, introducing Brian to Robert Fraser and Christopher Gibbs and the rest of the circle as the 'leader of the Rolling Stones'.

The Stones and these hip aristos were a perfect match for each other. The Stones came away from the encounter with a patina of aristocratic decadence that served as a perfect counterfoil to the raw roots blues of their music. It suffuses their classic albums from *Beggars Banquet* to *Exile on Main Street*, and it transformed the Stones from pop stars into cultural icons.

I began going round to Courtfield Road a year after Nicholas was born. I developed an irrepressible need to get out of the flat. I was bored, I felt trapped and I was exhausted. In the three years between Adrienne Posta's party where I met Andrew Oldham until I ran off with Mick Jagger, I made four singles and two albums, went on three tours, did six weeks in Paris at the Olympia, not to mention countless interviews, *Top of the Pops* and on and on.

Before I started working in pop music I was having a good time; going to parties, hanging about in coffee bars, the usual seventeen-year-old stuff. Nice as it was to be 'discovered' and become a pop star, I couldn't shake the feeling that I had missed something. My marriage to John had been a shotgun wedding naturally; in 1965 if you got pregnant you got married. Our honeymoon, although spent in Paris, was anything but conventional. The only people we saw during the week were Allen Ginsberg and Lawrence Ferlinghetti. Great slangy, mantra-slathering beatniks careening around our hotel room, throwing up, spilling cheap rosé all over the place and ranting on about the Rosenbergs, Rimbaud, Tangier and buggery. We also ran into Gregory Corso, whose idea of breakfast was to mix up a Brompton Cocktail – half morphine and half cocaine – and pass out on the floor of the Hotel Louisiana.

You might reasonably ask why we were sharing our honeymoon suite with a bunch of drug-addled beatnik poets, but I didn't. Mostly we were doing it because it was what John wanted to do, and of course it was wonderful. But life back home at Lennox Gardens was more of the same, John's idea of a normal routine was to put liquid methedrine in his coffee in the morning before going off to work at the Indica Bookshop with Miles. The bookshop was on the ground floor and John's gallery was in the basement.

My exquisitely decorated nest had turned into a crash pad for talented layabouts, American junkies, actually. This was when you could still get British pharmaceutical heroin legally, and that was the principal reason all these guys came to London. Mad types like Mason Hoffenberg would show up at our house and end up staying for months at a time. Mason had popped in to see John for a few days around Christmas the previous year, and the following May he was still there, draped about the house and conked out in various states of stupefaction. He was a wicked mimic with an undepletable store of salty anecdotes. An enormously funny man – he had written *Candy* with Terry Southern – and wonderfully good company. I might have found it all a lot more amusing if I had been allowed to join in, but at the start I didn't smoke, drink or do drugs, and that's just the way John liked it. Life was quietly becoming nightmarish.

I would get up in the morning, there'd be no heat. I'd have to step over several people crashed in the living room. I'd go into the kitchen to warm up a bottle for Nicholas and find the draining board strewn with bloody needles. One morning I went round the whole flat and collected all these jacks, these little heroin pills, hidden all over the place – there were hundreds of them – and I flushed them down the toilet. I just couldn't take it any more. But I stuck it out for two years, trying to lead my normal middle-class life as best I could for as long as I could. In this bohemian, druggie household I had been badly miscast as mother-angel-girlfriend-wife and blessed Virgin Mary. An unsufferable role that I finally began to hate with a passion. I was bored, I was lonely, I had begun to find John and his cerebral junkies tiresome, and all around me was the centrifugal whirl of the sixties. I wanted to see what all the fuss was about.

I've always liked going out on my own – I can manoeuvre better, and that's just what I started to do. I'd leave John at home with Nicholas and the nanny, his drugs and his friends, and I'd go off to my drugs and my friends. I loved getting dressed up and putting on my make-up with John quietly fuming. He knew he couldn't really stop me from going out, but that didn't stop him from trying. One night he threw all my jars of make-up against the wall. That was actually one of the main reasons I left him!

Jealousy played little part in all this. John mainly objected to my extravagance; every time I left the house I would spend an absolute fortune. Sure, I kept the house going but everything else I made – and I made a lot of money – I spent on myself. I was mean and I was petty when it came to money. John was running an art gallery and when it went bust, I didn't lift a finger to help. I didn't behave like a human being at all. I was a shopping addict; my first really serious addiction.

My first stop of the evening was always Brian and Anita's. Keith Richards practically lived there too; he and Brian were fast friends in those days. Every day Keith would walk all the way from his flat in St John's Wood to Gloucester Road, about four miles. After he broke up with Linda Keith, his girlfriend at the time, he took to spending even more time there. Supposedly he no longer had a place to stay, but I always suspected it was to get closer to Anita. Keith just exuded lonely bachelorhood, and naturally Brian and Anita always let him crash there.

The Courtfield Road flat itself was a grungy place. Mattress on the floor, sink piled high with dirty dishes, posters half falling down. But Christopher had insisted Anita buy it. 'You simply have to get it, darling. With a little tarting up it could be absolutely ravishing.' And of course it could have been. It was your classic artist's studio; high ceilings, skylights, huge windows and one very large room with a winding staircase up to a minstrels' gallery.

The place had definite possibilities, but we all knew that absolutely nothing was ever going to be done. During the entire time Brian and Anita lived there it remained exactly as it was the day they moved in, with the exception of a few sticks of furniture and a couple of bizarre, moth-eaten stuffed animals from a film Anita had made in Germany.

Brian would sit on the floor, very high, and tell you what it was going to look like when he got it together. Anita and Brian were like two beautiful children who had inherited a decrepit palazzo. Every day they would dress up in their furs, satins and velvets and parade about and invite people over, and we would all sit on the floor and talk about the fantastic things we would do with the kingdom if only we could.

There were two secret rooms, which added to the flat's playhouse quality. A room below the kitchen that you got to through a hatch in the floor, and an attic that you reached by means of a metal ladder you could pull down. This attic was a wonderful gothic-looking storage space where books and clothes and Brian's train magazines were stored.

A couple of times I dropped by Courtfield Road and found Brian there all by himself. He invited me in with a flourish. Brian had lovely manners and a little whispery voice. He was so intelligent and would become very animated when the subject interested him. Trains, Ingmar Bergman movies, anything magical. Like a lot of people at the time, myself included, he was convinced there was a mystic link between druidic monuments and flying saucers. Extraterrestrials were going to read these signs from their spaceship windows and get the message. It was the local credo: Glastonbury, ley lines and intelligent life in outer space. I've forgotten exactly what it was we believed, but we believed it fiercely! And if little green men were going to contact anybody on the planet it would have to be us, wouldn't it?

In the middle of one of these conversations, Brian began coming on to me out of the clear blue. I had the oddest feeling he was simply being polite. I was in his flat, I was a pretty girl . . . and he was a Rolling Stone, making it almost *de rigueur* that he make a pass at me, it was the new sexual politesse.

For my part, I thought, Oh, he's making a play for me. I really should let him. I imagined that was what a flower child did. Hippie etiquette. You just sort of went along, didn't you?

I didn't really fancy Brian, and I was truly terrified of Anita. But Anita, unfortunately, was away and Brian and I, needless to say, were both very high. So after several large spliffs and what I gathered was courtship patter (involving the *Flying Scotsman*, Mary Wells, William Morris wallpaper and Tantric art) Brian led me up the little staircase to the minstrels' gallery. We lay down on a mattress and he unbuttoned my blouse. But after a bit of groping about, it just fizzled out. He was a wonderfully feeble guy, quite incapable of real sex. And, of course, he was doing a lot of Mandrax, which rendered him even more wobbly than he already was. Brian only had so much energy.

Every once in a while, Mick would drop in at Courtfield Road. Very fastidious always, with an absolute horror of bohemian living. The sink full of dirty dishes so appalled him he could never stay long. Mick's visits were of an almost proprietorial nature, he'd come by to inspect everything, see that all was going along well with the Firm, smoke a joint and split.

Mick and Brian were always far more interested in the power shifts in the group than Keith, but of course it was whoever allied himself with Keith who would have the power. The balance in the group was completely different from what it was later to become. The guitar players, Brian and Keith, were inseparable, with Mick and Andrew Oldham off in the other corner. They were all quite far from Their Satanic Majesties or whatever it is they are supposed to have become. Their personae were gradually forming out of a blend of blues mythology and King's Road *noblesse oblige*. Like boys, playing in suits of armour shortly before a voice out of the clouds comes and tells them, 'Thou shalt be Princes of Darkness.'

One of the great attractions of Courtfield Road for me was getting high. I'd only recently started smoking hash but I couldn't smoke at home because John – an incredible piece of drug chauvinism this – wouldn't permit me to. People were shooting up all over the house and I wasn't allowed to roll a joint! I never actually went to John and said, 'let me try what you're doing, let me have a joint', because I knew damn well John would never go for it. It was a men's club that I couldn't join. I was the wife and the mother and the golden goose, the one making the money to buy this stuff they were all doing. It was me doing three gigs a night in Manchester and coming back with thousands of pounds – in cash. John wasn't going to mess that up.

The entertaining at Courtfield Road was of the most basic kind. Joint-rolling, mainly. Endless joint-rolling. It was still quite a novelty and we would smoke until we were obliterated. Really fascinating stuff when you're eighteen. Every thought twined about itself so many times there was no way of articulating it, so very little was ever said.

It's such a hoot this 'twas-the-night-before-Christmas fustian in which Terry Southern now writes about this time: 'Gambolling about Old Smoke, I warrant, as young lovers are wont.' I don't remember him speaking this way at all, or anybody else for that matter, but in retrospect it all becomes very gothic and I suppose it was a bit like that – or should have been.

At about ten o'clock at night everyone would be

famished and we'd stagger out to Alvaro's for some

wonderful pasta. But once we got there we'd be so stoned we could barely manage more than a mouthful. I'd stare at the exquisite china and watch the tiny dragons crawl over the fettuccine while Anita and Robert talked about shoes and art in Italian.

One of the best things about visiting Anita and Brian was watching them get ready to go out. What a scene! They were both dauntless shoppers and excessively vain. Hours and hours were spent putting on clothes and taking them off again. Heaps of scarves, hats, shirts and boots flew out of drawers and trunks. Unending trying on of outfits, primping and sashaying. They were beautiful, they were the spitting image of each other and not an ounce of modesty existed between the two of them. I would sit mesmerized for hours, watching them preening in the mirror, trying on each other's clothes. All roles and gender would evaporate in these narcissistic performances, where Anita would turn Brian into the Sun King, Françoise Hardy or the mirror image of herself.

She loved him very much, but there was some ugly stuff going on between them. There were often bruises on her arms. No one ever said anything, what would there be to say? We all knew it was

Brian. Anita is not the sort of feminine, confiding person who invites speculation into her private life. It would have been a point of honour on her part not to say anything. Anita wanted at all costs to be considered invincible. She always seemed to know exactly what she was doing.

I think I knew very clearly how to detach even then. We were all doing so many drugs – hash and LSD mostly – you had to be a bit careful what you focused on or you would become completely obsessed. It sounds a bit brutal, but as long as I wasn't the one being beaten up I didn't care. I was very, very self-involved, and I was walking a fucking tightrope myself.

When I first met Brian, he was on one of his brief upswings, but even during this manic phase a doomed look began to set in his face. Inner demons had started eating away at that Renaissance angel's head.

Whatever was wrong with Brian had begun a long time before; you have only to look at childhood pictures of Mick, Keith and Brian to see it. After looking at snapshots of a little cheerful Mick and a strong, very tough little Keith, suddenly to come upon Brian's baby picture is quite startling. A jowly, miserable child is looking up at you with exactly that expression of helpless victimization he gave off in the last year of his life.

Brian was a mess – neurasthenic and hypersensitive. Twitchy. The slightest thing would set him off. He would let things gnaw at him and he would brood. This paranoiac condition worsened, naturally, on acid. Everybody would be laughing and looning about, and Brian would be over in the corner all crumpled up. It's Anita's belief that Brian never recovered from his first trip. Acid and pills only worsened his condition and compounded his paranoia into a full-blown persecution mania. But he embraced his horrors, as if on acid he was finally able to confront his afflictions in a palpable form.

Drowning voices in the pipes, traffic noises turning into sinister conversations. We've all heard these things on acid. Nevertheless, it's not too cool to announce that your appliances are plotting against you, but for Brian these thoughts were so incessant that he couldn't help himself. Brian simply verbalized what everyone else was thinking. Things I, for one, was thinking. But these outbursts left him open to ridicule, and they all taunted him.

Keith would ask: 'It's the snakes again, is it,

Brian?' Then to us in a stage whisper: 'The snakes in the wiring, they're talking to Brian.' Gales of laughter.

Poor Brian was somewhat uncool. He could summon coolness up, but fundamentally he wasn't cool at all. His was a false cool. Keith, on the other hand, really was cool, ice cool, always. He hasn't changed at all, he's become more and more strange looking and developed this grand desperado carapace, but inside, Keith is not unlike his twenty-two-year-old self. He has a wickedly twisted sense of humour that on acid could become quite diabolical. We'd be out on the balcony and he'd whisper to Anita: 'Go on, darling, jump why don't you?' But she would turn with that wonderful smile of hers and tell him: 'You little fucker, what are you trying to do?'

Keith was gorgeous in those days. When I think how he looked, how beautiful he was – and pure. Long before I got to know him, I had a huge crush on him. For years. He was the epitome of my ideal of the tortured Byronic soul, it was quite clear even then that he was a genius. He isn't a bit shy now, but when I first met him he was agonizingly shy and painfully introverted. He didn't talk at all. I mean all that stuff that Mick did, like trying to make me sit on his lap, Keith would rather have died than do anything like that.

Mick and Keith both developed their tabloid personae while they were on the road. Mick became the grand seigneur and the great gentleman, and Keith developed this bravado. The pirate who sailed with Captain Kidd. Arrr!

Brian could be so irritating on acid, even more irritating than usual. Agitated, fidgety, a coil of strung-out energy. The mad pace of a haywire inner clock. Manic scribbling in notebooks followed by pages being ripped out. Then the frantic business with the tapes would start. Recording, erasing, recording, erasing. Reels unspooling all over the floor, the offending tapes being hurled across the room. These were Brian's phantom songs. After working in this way with Brian, it must have been such a relief for Keith to go back to working with Mick. It wasn't going anywhere. Out of all the frenetic activity that went on, only one song emerged during the entire time I was going to Courtfield Road and that was 'Ruby Tuesday'. It was Brian's swan song. At one point he began to paint a mural of a graveyard on the wall behind the bed – just 23 above the pillows was a large headstone. He never got around to writing his name on it, but you knew that the headstone was for him.

Today you would put anybody in Brian's shaky condition straight into hospital. But we never even considered it. I don't honestly think it crossed anybody's mind to 'seek professional help'. And he, of course, would never have accepted it. We saw ourselves as the vanguard of the new era. The admission that one of the élite was mentally unbalanced might have endangered the whole Children's Crusade before it had even got started. The fact that Brian was a self-indulgent and brittle monster didn't help in eliciting sympathy when he began to unravel.

I remember one particularly harrowing scene. There was no bell at Courtfield Road, so in order to get into the flat you had to shout up. Brian or Anita would throw the keys down or come and open the door. One day we were all at the flat, Keith, Brian, Anita, me and one or two other people. We were all quite stoned and suddenly we heard people outside on the pavement calling up, but it wasn't the usual hippie growl, 'Brian, open the fucking door, man!' It was two troubled-sounding voices, a man's and a woman's. We all went out on the balcony to see who it was.

There down below was Brian's old girlfriend with her two-year-old baby, Julian, and her father. She was raising the baby up in the air in a classic gesture of supplication, asking Brian for help, begging him. She wanted child support and the baby was very obviously Brian's. 'It's your kid, Brian, you know it is. We're really in a bad way, we need some help. Please!' All with the father chiming in: 'You bloody do the right thing by her, boy, you hear!'

Brian and Anita just peered down on them as if they were some inferior species. Foppish aristocrats in their finery jeering at the *sans culottes* below. Upstairs everyone was laughing about it. It was so appalling, like something out of a Mexican folk tale, but Anita and Brian seemed to enjoy every minute of it.

Colston Hall

There were lots of things I could have done at the age of nineteen that would have been more healthy than becoming Mick Jagger's inamorata. In the end it doesn't matter that hearts got broken and that we sweated blood. Maybe the most you can expect from a relationship that goes bad is to come out of it with a few good songs.

It all began quite inauspiciously with a casual invitation from Brian and Keith to see the Stones play at Colston Hall in Bristol. I was driven down in my new Mustang, Mustang Sally (the Wilson Pickett song had just come out). Keith and Brian met me at the stage door and took me backstage. Ike and Tina Turner were on the same bill, and in the hallway outside the Stones' dressing room Mick was being taught to dance the Sideways Pony by Tina Turner (much to the amusement of the Ikettes). Mick could dance, but compared to Tina he was, well, spastic. Black dance steps weren't

something that came to him easily, so learning the

Sideways Pony was for Mick like learning a *pas de deux*. He is English, after all.

'On the two, honey, on the two,' Tina would demonstrate a few steps and Mick would try to follow. 'Let's try it again. One, two, three four five . . . God! Mick, you're scaring me!'

Brian and Keith were standing in a corner giggling (and not exactly trying to hide it). They were bluesmen from England's mental delta, and thought Mick was a jerk for getting so intense about the dance step stuff – showbiz fluff that the real musos would despise. But it didn't rattle Mick at all, he was very good humoured about the whole thing. When Tina rolled her eyeballs at Mick's flat-footedness, he put his hand to his head in mock desperation and said, 'Does this mean I won't be black in the next life?'

Tina replied, 'Are you sure you want to be?'

After Ike and Tina went on, I stood backstage . . . watching Mick watching Tina. Then I decided to go and see the rest of the show from the front. Such a blast of energy! Their flawless mix of precision and funk erupting like a tropical heat wave in this dreary port. The people in the audience got into Ike and Tina okay, they felt the heat, they moved, they wiggled and jiggled. But in a strange way it didn't touch them personally, it was a novelty thing.

When the Stones came on, it was another story altogether. The audience caught fire. I had been on many tours and seen a lot of groups drive audiences crazy – but this was something I'd never seen. It was on another level entirely. Darker, more fanatical, and vaguely menacing.

Almost from the first notes of 'I'm A King Bee', an unearthly howl went up from thousands of possessed teenagers. Girls began pulling out their hair, standing on the backs of their seats, pupils dilating, shaking uncontrollably. It was as if they were on some strange drug that propelled and synchronized them. Snake-handling frenzy buzzed through the hall, cases of clinical Dionysian mass hysteria were breaking out everywhere. Mick effortlessly reached inside them and snapped that twig, he knew exactly how to locate the North Africa of the teenage cranium. I was an infidel at a ceremony that only those of the true faith could fathom, I had lost all my bearings. I was on a beach in Tunisia surrounded by cannibalistic urchins, I was in the *Village of the Damned* unable to think of a brick wall. But I felt in no danger, since I was, of course, quite invisible. It was not me they wished to tear limb from limb, it was Mick. Mick was their Dionysus, he was the dancing god.

While the other Stones stood rooted mono-lithically to the ground like Easter Island statues, Mick whirled about the stage. A slinky mod Frankenstein monster – lurching, jerking, writhing, convulsing – like a marionette being zapped every few seconds by a jolt of electricity. Through these contortions he flawlessly telegraphed the whole Stones' posture – swaggering, sullen, arrogant, androgynous. You got it entirely from Mick's danc-ing, since the band was made all but inaudible by the ululating teenage girls.

After the concert my roadie went off in the Mustang and I stayed on at the Ship Hotel. I didn't book a room, I just went up to Mick's with Brian and Keith. Michael Cooper was working for Roman Polanski at the time and he'd brought down a print of *Repulsion*, the film Polanski had just finished edit-ing. This was Michael's great talent, making all the connections – Polanski, the Stones, the hip aristos, pop artists. It was at just that point before the Stones became the be-all and end-all. It was all still so hip 29 that only Michael, Robert and Christopher really knew.

We all sat around and watched *Repulsion*. I smoked many joints and became extremely stoned. I was speechless and unable to move. Everybody was quite high, and the film was so strange that we all watched it in a reverent silence.

There were a lot of girls in the room and there was a rather obvious business going on over who was going to sleep with whom. People began pairing off. One by one they all left to go to bed or hooked with someone or got bored and wandered out until then there was just this one other girl and myself left in the room with Mick. She was an Ikette and she really sat it out. I was still sitting there, I think, because I couldn't move. And anyway I didn't have anywhere to go: my car had gone, I told myself, I hadn't booked a room, you know, that type of thing. Eventually the Ikette got up and left. I was left with Mick and that, as they say, was that.

We started chatting about Roman Polanski. I heard myself saying that I thought Polanski was a 'magus'. The words just hung in the air, the way they do when you're stoned. After a long pause

Mick said: 'It's one of the things I'm quite interested in right now.'

'Excuse me?'

'Oh, you know, disturbed states of mind, that kind of thing.'

'Hmmm . . . what do you mean, exactly?' I'd learned this from John: if you don't understand something you insist they define their terms.

'Oh, you know, the pressures of modern life, people going off the deep end.'

'Like Bob Dylan . . .'

'Yeah, but that's his speciality isn't it, Desolation Row? We're just strolling past Bedlam, we don't actually live there yet.'

It was already dawn. We'd been circling each other that long, but I still didn't know what I really wanted to do. I found that moment where you're about to have sex so difficult, always have. So to put it off a bit, I said, 'Let's go for a walk . . .' And we went out and walked about in a park that was near the hotel.

I didn't know Mick at all, and my way of ascertaining whether he was all right or just a jerk was to ask him a lot of questions about King Arthur.

'Do you remember the name of Arthur's sword?'

'Come forth from the stone, Excalibur! I practised that bit quite a lot actually in my back yard in Dartford using a wooden sword and a cardboard box.'

'Have you ever been to Stonehenge?'

'Yeah, went with my mum and dad when I was little. All I remember is a lot of grown ups standing around wondering how in the world did they get that up there?'

'Yes, but how did they do it, do you think?'

'Druidic Department of Works. Merlin, wasn't it? They say he was a crafty old bloke, transported the stones all the way from Wales by magic, but it probably just looked like magic, sort of prehistoric engineering. He thought it sounded better to say "Oh I did it with a wand" you know, than saying "the point of leverage of an object suspended above the angle of momentum . . ."'

I remember asking Mick if he happened to know anything about the Holy Grail, and I have to admit he ran with the ball.

'The Holy Grail . . . let's see . . . Joseph of Arimathea. Isn't he the one that lost the damn thing? Supposed to be still somewhere in England.'

'What was the name of that knight who Guinevere deserted King Arthur for?'

He paused and looked at me and grinned, 'Sir Lancelot du Lac, was it? Am I going to pass my A Level, Marianne? What do you think?'

It was quite ludicrous but that's how we were then. You would ask your date, 'Do you know Genet? Have you read *A Rebours*?' and if he said yes, you'd fuck.

It was sunrise and my boots had got wet in the dew. When we got back to the room I remember he unlaced my boots and put them to dry by the heat. He was sweet that night, I was completely moved by his kindness. And then we made love. And then I left. But, of course, I was beginning to think, 'This guy is pretty amazing!'

A few days later I took off for Italy. I'd rented a villa in Positano so Nicholas and I could spend a few weeks in the sun with his nanny, Diana. Pat, my roadie, came too of course. Just a couple of days before we left I ran into a black model, Kelly, in a boutique off Oxford Circus and we had a long chat. We liked each other immensely and quite on a whim I invited her to come with us. She paused for a few seconds then went home and packed.

On the way to Positano we stopped for a few days in Paris. Awaiting me was a heart-rending letter from John saying how wrong he'd been, begging me to come back. So uncharacteristic of him. The only way he could express those things he had never said the entire time we were married was to write them. Wonderful letter. I threw it out of the window.

After we'd been there a few days, Kelly asked if she could invite her boyfriend, who was in Paris. She told me he was a model, too, also American, and she thought I'd really get on with him. Of course. The boyfriend came, he was gorgeous and I did get on fabulously with him. The first night he was there we made love on the terrace under the stars. To this day Kelly has never spoken to me again. I don't blame her, I suppose, but it was Positano, there was a full moon, he was beautiful. In those days they were my idea of extenuating circumstances.

Upon arriving in Positano I had been quite flattered to find there was a stack of messages from Mick, and when Kelly left I had a lot of time on my hands to think about him. Something had been set in motion, but I wasn't quite sure what it was.

Although I loved being unattached, I was very frightened of it. My career was beginning to pall on me. 'Counting' was the record I had out at the time and I was thoroughly sick of it. I was going through one of those periods where I was seriously fed up with the whole business. This pop music thing had become a horrible millstone. It was just grinding on and on. One of the things I'm not very proud of (but which I know is true), is that I was looking for a way out of my life, and Mick presented me with it.

Here I was with little Nicholas, married to an unworldly man who never made a penny. I was supporting us all by myself – something I never much cared for. And here was Mick being very attentive, romantic and protective.

I remembered him coming round one winter with Andrew when I was living at Lennox Gardens. They dropped in for a cup of coffee. John had left and it was freezing cold; there was one little electric fire in the flat. I hardly knew Mick at this point and I could see he was incredibly shocked and actually touched by my living conditions. Being the great romantic he is and really was then . . . I could see he was the kind of man who could feel that stuff, 35 could see my plight. How terrible! What happens to a woman alone with her baby? I remember being amazed at how considerate he was, and that he would show it. John was never like that. He was much too cool, hip and arrogant to show his feelings.

But it was all incredibly odd, really, ending up with Mick. It was so out of character, I now realize, for him to choose me – given what I believed in and the way I was. Especially in comparison with what kind of woman he thought he was getting! Mick was under the illusion that I actually was the slightly dizzy, aristocratic, virginal child-troubadour that Andrew Oldham and Andy Wickham had invented. On the other hand, he might have known me better than I realized.

I heard somewhere that Mick had actually wanted Julie Christie, and when he couldn't get her, he settled for me. Who knows where that came from! Yet somehow it sounds quite real to me. It has to do with Mick's Dolly Fixation and goes back, no doubt, to the image of me that Andrew had created. I remember being surprised that Mick didn't see straight through it.

Mick could be wonderfully nice when he wanted to be, and I really thought I wanted to be with someone who would pamper me for a change. Living with John had been very trying because of, well, the way he was. He was incredibly selfish. Coming directly from this scene, I thought Mick was a genuine haven. Mick was affectionate, interesting, funny and very attentive. He called me constantly. He wasn't fucked up like Brian, he didn't do drugs. You could actually lead a life with Mick and, let's face it, there was no way I could have got off my treadmill if I hadn't become involved with Mick. Once I became Mick's girlfriend I no longer had to work, not for the money anyway. I could do *The Three Sisters* for just £18 a week and not give a damn.

I had brought one of the Stones' records with me to Italy, *High Tide and Green Grass*, which I played a lot. And I wonder if I didn't almost talk myself into Mick, the way you can, you know, with love. Invent it and then put it into practice. Every time I put on *High Tide and Green Grass*, Mick would call. It was uncanny. Perhaps it really was fate, I began to tell myself. I didn't have the wit to think things through. I couldn't imagine asking myself, 'Well, what could be the disadvantages of this?' I never gave it a thought. And why should I? Did anybody?

Still . . . from the very beginning, one part of me knew that I was involving myself in a somewhat curious situation. He and Andrew Oldham were birds of a feather. He was camp and he wore make-up at a time when this was still very unusual. I had an inkling that there was a sexual undercurrent between them.

I think I knew in some part of my mind that Mick was bisexual, as well. But what I somehow thought that meant was that he would be nicer to me. 'Real men' scared me, but Andrew didn't, and Mick felt safe and easy to be around.

Anyway, I must have had some misgivings about Mick because I remember calling Allen Klein, the Stones' new business manager, from Positano and telling him about Mick and confessing to him that I was really in love with Keith. I had only met Allen a couple of times, but I liked him at once and trusted his judgement. Allen made the situation simple: 'But, Marianne, if you go with Keith it'll destroy Mick.' And he was right, it would have been devastating, but it's also true that the whole time I was with Mick I was in love with Keith. And so in this way, I too was drawn into the web.

I flew back from Positano and left Diana, Pat and

Nicholas to drive the Mustang back across the Alps. It was a nightmare! The damn car broke down, there were no parts, it took ages for them to get back. I'd been away for a couple of months and on my first night back in London I checked into the Mayfair Hotel. This was a night out. I was free.

I went up to my room and called Brian's flat. Anita was away. Brian, Keith and Tara were there. They were delighted to hear from me, and said they would be over to fetch me in a matter of minutes. I thought they wanted to be with me because I was such fun and one of them. Of course, they were wondering when and if they were going to have sex with me. That's the way things go. So they came over, picked me up and we all went back to Brian's flat where we promptly took acid. It was very good acid, Brian had got it from Robert who had got it from the CIA in California.

Keith, Brian and Tara lay around on sofas in exquisite clothes from various raids on Hung On You, Granny Takes A Trip and the Chelsea Antique Market. Euphoria took over as the acid came on. How astonishing they all look, I thought, just before truly drastic alterations began to take place. Every thought I had took on a physical dimension, molecules breaking up. One rarely gets to see one's friends in such detail. Subatomically. Great! It's something I've always hoped I'd be granted: second sight. Nothing was hidden from me, they were becoming transparent as if I'd put on x-ray specs. Their true natures were being bared, their spirit selves. And, along with this – almost simultaneously – I saw enactments of their past lives. Tiny, mercurial operas. They, Keith, Brian, Tara – I was not surprised to learn – had existed throughout history.

In these soul genealogies Brian appeared as Pan, an urbane satyr in crushed velvet, horned, goat-legged. A voluptuous, overripe god gone to seed. Not Pan himself, exactly, more a foppish noble play-ing a faun at the court of Versailles. Blowing on his reed pipe, silhouetted against a painted wild mountain backdrop. A debauched aristocrat pursu-ing a flock of diaphanously clothed peasant girls dressed as nymphs . . . But Pan is out of breath, and reaches for his inhaler.

Now Keith as Byron: the injured, tormented, doomed Romantic hero, with wild hair and gaunt visage. Not Byron the hooray, the upper-class dilettante, musing on a crepuscular sky at Sunium. Darker, more alive, an eruptive, restless presence violently bursting through. Byron as punk, a fusion of decadence and surging energy. Rock raunch, hipster cool and I-don't-give-a-fuck defiance deftly grafted on the languid world-weary pose of Romantic agony.

Where Brian was soft, malleable, vague and unstable, everything about Keith was angular, flinty, compact, distinct. The hatchet face, chiselled, rock-hard features, Indian scout's eyes that bore through everything. The mysterious rider appearing out of nowhere, hypnotic, sinister, disturbing. Cursed-by-fate intensity, set off against gorgeous clothes, self-mocking humour and a sardonic turn of phrase.

Tara Browne was pure courtier. He had none of Keith's incredible life force pulsing through him. I'd known Tara for a long time. He'd just split up with his wife, Nikki, who had spent most of their marriage having affairs with hunky Spanish guys in Marbella. Tara was very unhappy at the time and he was looking for someone. He liked me and since he was a Guinness heir I also knew that he must be very, very rich. But there was no strength there, no direct current. The Stones were the true aristocracy here and Tara faded in comparison.

Through the acid haze I soon became aware that the atmosphere was very sexually charged . . . and that I was the only woman in the room. It just buzzed in the air for a while, a sort of static electricity. And then Brian, being the most insecure and out of it, came over to claim me. I was even less attracted to him this time than I had been before, but I was unable in those days to say no to anybody. Luckily, people were so scared of me that very few passes were made at all. I imagined he was Pan in sheepskins and I was the moon-goddess, Selene. We went up to the minstrels' gallery. I wasn't worried about the others because I knew they were tripping off into some other space. In a way, our tryst was like a scene from an Elizabethan play where the lovers retire to a bower represented by a painted cloth. Brian and I diddled about a bit, but it was ridiculous (even on a mythological level). Leaning over me . . . a weary, asthmatic god.

At some point I felt uncomfortable and *de trop*. Perhaps it was Brian's weirdness, perhaps I was just exhausted, but I began to feel really strange. I knew that I'd be happier on my own. I wanted to experience my trip as intensely as possible. Obviously there was much more to LSD than letting Brian Jones touch my breasts. That was the dull bit! I wanted to be in the seclusion of my own house, see visions, commune with the cosmos, dissolve into bright little molecules and travel through space. I knew I could do this much better at home. By this point the Mayfair Hotel had begun to seem dauntingly adult, so I crept out and made my way back to Lennox Gardens.

I lay down on the bed, but sleep was out of the question. I found that when I shut my eyes I could see right through my eyelids. My tastefully decorated bedroom was showing signs of mental unbalance. Even the stolid Sanderson wallpaper became animated. The cabbage roses on the trellis did a little dance. I was surprised I'd never noticed that each of those roses had a distinct personality, like fat little ballerinas doing a lumbering *pas de deux* across my wall. It was obvious that the designer must have had this in mind when he created the pattern. He was sending out a message that only a few, very few would ever get, like an inscription found in a pharaoh's tomb that would unlock the secrets of the universe. Hidden in the wallpaper, how perfect! I would never look at this wall again in quite the same way.

A breeze blew in through the window. The wallpaper ballet gave way to a more spectacular performance as the heavy purple curtains billowed in the wind. They were wool and the light shone through them. In an instant, a huge Cocteau line drawing of Orpheus the height and breadth of the window flashed through the room. It began to tremble like the threads of a cobweb and then another Cocteau drawing traced itself over that one, and another, and another, until the room was filled with swooping black lines, arabesques looping and spinning.

I was being borne along on the incessant tide of fantastic images, really losing myself in the surrealistic scribbling rolling before my eyes. When the phone rang I answered it in the spirit of 'whatever it is, I can handle it.' Always a mistake on acid. It was Keith.

'Where did you go, Marianne? We looked everywhere for you,' he said urgently, like someone adrift on a raft.

'Oh darling, I was feeling a bit out of it and I –'

'But you can't just abandon ship like that! You don't know what your leaving did to the . . . uh . . .' Apparently I had done something to the mystic bond.

'Oh, how awful of me!' I said.

'We mustn't disconnect,' Keith insisted, 'everything depends on it. The group has to stay together.' Keith must have been bored or something. And those funny feelings you get when someone goes off on their own in the middle of a trip. Although it wasn't as if we had all been doing things together while I was there. Evidently the sacred vibrations had been perturbed, and I had been well trained by John not to upset the vibe. People tripping were to be treated as gingerly as vials of nitroglycerine.

'Oh right, darling, I'll be right over.'

I told Keith I didn't have a farthing to my name and he said he'd meet the cab downstairs and pay the driver. But when I got to Courtfield Road we didn't stay; Keith got into the cab with me.

'Brian passed out and Tara's gone home. Let's go back to your hotel.'

That was the night I ended up with Keith. It was a wonderful night of sex. As a matter of fact, that night with Keith was the best night I've ever had in my life. Although I did, of course, know Keith a great deal better than I knew Mick I still had to ask him that all-important question.

'Darling . . .'

'Yes?'

'What do you think ever happened to the Holy Grail?'

'What? The Holy bloody Grail? Christ, Marianne, are you still tripping?'

As dawn came up over London I put on *The Four Seasons*. It was sublime. I was in heaven. I had always been in love with Keith, but very shyly. Now I was totally bowled over. Next day I was fluttering around in a state of absolute rapture.

'Oh, darling,' I say to Keith, 'that was such a night!'

Keith is pulling on his boots and, out of the blue, he pauses, cocks his head and says: 'You know who really has it bad for you, don't you?'

'Oh, no, darling, who's that?'

'Mick! Didn't you know?'

'Well . . . I . . . he does call me now and then.'

'Oh, he's smitten all right, Marianne.'

'Is he, really?'

'Go on, love, give him a jingle, he'll fall off his

chair. He's not that bad when you get to know him, you know.'

I was speechless. Again. He was telling me that I shouldn't bother with him. I should pursue Mick, instead. It was so awful, I was crushed. He set me up and I simply accepted it as a *fait accompli*: 'Oh, all right. I see, Mick and Marianne. I think that's what I'll do then.' I'd been given my role. Incredible, isn't it? It's all these funny things you do when you're young and on acid. I thought Keith was perfection, but I didn't think I was exceptional or glamorous enough for him.

And then . . . off he went! He never said a word to anybody about our night together and neither did I. It just stayed there, this perfect night.

I wish now I'd had the strength to say, 'Fuck Mick, man. I like you.' It's something I could summon up now, but in those days it was totally beyond my range. Not that it would have helped. I was being given the brush-off.

I knew Mick would be kind to me. Keith was a much more dangerous entity, really, more mysterious. Maybe it was all for the best.

Anita was still with Brian when I spent the night with Keith. Keith and I were on our own, but I knew in my heart of hearts that Keith was in love with Anita. I could just feel that whatever he wanted, I wasn't it. I was too English and too conventional for him. The signals I was picking up were accurate, he was already obsessed.

It's really very odd, the whole business: Keith and Anita, Mick and me. The magic, the alchemy of the alliances was powerful and had an impact far beyond our little romances. I don't, obviously, know why. I've always been extremely wary of Kenneth Anger and the Tower and all the dark stuff. But there was definitely something very powerful psychically about my alliance with Mick. It enhanced us both in a way that, in the end, almost destroyed me.

PENGUIN 60s